Finglas Way 1

Ken Duffy

Copyright © 2020 Ken Duffy
All rights reserved.

Dedicated to me Ma

Me Ma, she was the best I say
Slogging her guts out, every day
You know, what I say is true
Cause your Ma, was the same too

Give you the bread, from her mouth
All Ma's did, I have no doubt
Rising early, a long day's work ahead
Make me breakfast, get me out of bed

Galtee sambo's, made for me lunch
In the schoolyard, there I would munch
Wash me laundry, mended and stitched
Repaired me clothes, they weren't ditched

Scrimped and scraped, doing her best
Trying to cope, just like all the rest
Thanks Ma, those memories won't fade
Miss you still, I wish you had stayed

Table of Contents

Introduction	7
Finglas Way Back When	9
The Silverspoon	11
Down the Chariot Hills	12
Gateaux, Jeyes and Butterkrust	15
Smell of Horse Shit	16
Butterkrust on the Jamestown	18
Building Site Battles	21
Finglas Shamrock	22
The Drake Inn	24
Cream on Top	26
Tin Church at Cappagh	29
The Christmas Feast	30
Frozen Milk Bottles	33
Tree Climbing	34
Swings on Lampposts	36
Animal Mad	38
Cabra Baths	40
Caps for me Gun	42
Escaping Reality	45
Going on the Mitch	46
Let's Play Pretend	49
Me Bedroom Fortress	50

A Scout Never to Be	53
Summer Holliers	54
Me Favorite Toy	56
A Bad Education	59
Finglas Olympians	60
Bareback Twins	63
At the Cappagh Crossing	64
Sweets I Loved to Eat	66
Ma's Sisters and Brothers	69
Enniskerry Weekends	70
Slave to 70's Fashion	72
Snow Games	75
The Finglas Mammy	77
Mad About the Flicks	78
Music Growing Up	80
Bottler is Gone	83
Ode to Phil Lynott	84
Help the Halloween Party	87
'Twas Christmas	88
Thanks	90

Introduction

I have great memories of growing up in Finglas as a child. Now I'm not saying everything was cosy and rosy in the garden, sure whose childhood was? Life was hard for our parents, they struggled, but always managed to come up trumps for us when it mattered.

I remember fondly all the outdoor and indoor games we played as kids, the friendships made, the adventures we would go on with our gang, our summer holidays, (now called staycations). All these memories have been my inspiration for writing this book. I hope you get the same enjoyment reading it as I have had writing it.

I hope my book succeeds in transporting you back. That it reactivates your childhood memories, helps you to relive that very special time in your life. A time of play, before the responsibility of adult life.

The past year has been a very difficult time for everyone dealing with the Covid-19 pandemic. Some of you have lost loved ones to it, to you I send my heartfelt condolences for your loss.

I would like to take this opportunity to wish everyone a safe journey into 2021 and into the years beyond, be safe and be happy.

Finglas Way Back When

Finglas Way Back When

Kids running wild, visit me head
Van shop, where we got our bread
Take home a dog, found as a stray
Begging the ma, please can it stay

Mad adventures, out with me mates
Make a sleigh, out of wooden crates
Xmas dinners, cooked by me Mam
Toys from Santa, turkey and ham

Barber visits, when hair needed chop
No fancy stylists, to shape your mop
People bought fags, lose or in a pack
Put it on me slate, payday I'll be back

Walking to school, few cars in sight
Messing with pals, pretending to fight
Life was uncomplicated, simpler then
We were happy with little, way back when

The Silverspoon

The Silverspoon river, in its heyday
Was a kids mecca, our place of play
So many stories, that could be told
Memories of adventures, it does hold

Catching pinkeens, a jam jar in hand
On riverbank, with friends we'd stand
Remove shoes and socks, get feet wet
See how many pinkeens, we could net

Hedge lined roads, fields on each side
Over the bridge, long tested and tried
Between Cabra and Finglas, it did run
Silverspoon provided, a lot of our fun

In summer, we practically lived there
A water oasis, a place of go on I dare
We basked, taking in the sun's rays
Do kids enjoy it, like us in the old days

Down the Chariot Hills

As a kid, I played down the Chariot Hills
The craic was mighty, as were the thrills
Knock for me pals, get the gang together
Time for adventure, no matter the weather

From Plunkett Road, head down the alley
Towards the river, walk along the valley
An adventure in itself, just getting there
Us having the craic, a bit of go on I dare

Stuff used for slope slides, was mad I say
What imagination, used in our daily play
A piece of cardboard, protecting our arse
Sliding down that hill, was a comedy farse

Car bonnets, made for a mighty slide
Three or four on it, made a scary ride
Reach the bottom, we race back to the top
Repeated over, until darkness put a stop

glas Way Back When

Gateaux, Jeyes and Butterkrust

On McKee Ave, was Gateaux and Jeyes
Big Finglas employers, back in the days
Plenty a household, relied on their wage
A few relations, worked there at one stage

Me mum worked in both, over the years
Leaving home, her sweet little dears
Gateaux made cakes, of varying kinds
What will Ma bring, played on our minds

Jeyes made Jeyes Fluid, and other stuff
Us we preferred, a Gateaux's Cream Puff
Butterkrust Bakery, on Jamestown Road
Bread for dogs, Da got by the sack load

With the bread, Da got returned cake
Once a week, the journey he did make
For a time, we all lived in cake heaven
How many enjoyed it, me plus seven

Smell of Horse Shit

Merville Dairy, near Glasnevin hill
On Finglas Road, I can picture it still
Many me kin, entered that yard
Me Da and his Da, clocked their card

Some worked the dairy, some the road
Vehicles laden, with their milk load
Both sides of me family, worked on site
Duffy's and Duignan's, day and night

Me third generation, on the Duffy side
A family track record, tested and tried
Merville is gone, now a memory past
Sure nothing in life, was meant to last

Apartment blocks, now stand in place
Celtic Tiger, gave Merville a new face
Dairy employed, people far and wide
Many communities, for a wage relied

Different times, everything low tech
We were happy, not a mental wreck
Simple days, and memories to go with
Loading carts, the smell of horse shit

Butterkrust on the Jamestown

Butterkrust Bakery, on Jamestown Road
Baked bread and cakes, by the van load
Vans were parked, at the rear of the site
As lads we snuck in, under shade of night

Gran's back garden, bordered their fence
So did a hedge, that was thick and dense
It hid us well, as we crawled and snuck
Every so often, raised our heads to look

For us it was a game, a commando raid
It was scary stuff, yes we were afraid
A vans booty, was so finger licking
Returns of the day, made easy picking

Me mam never knew, nor did me dad
Of our evening raids, or cakes we had
Sure I couldn't help it, that is the truth
It was the blame, of an active sweet tooth

Building Site Battles

The Northway house, before its day
Was a building site, a place of play
Mounds of soil, and foundations deep
Made great trenches, or a castle keep

Hoarding placed, couldn't keep us out
During games, we'd holler and shout
Bang bang you're dead, now lay down
Building site, became a wild west town

War games, between Gerry and Yanks
Bigger boys, taking the higher ranks
Onward men, time to take that hill
Ducking, diving, many enemies to kill

Jumping a mound, to take some cover
As stench of death, in air did hover
I landed in water, up to me chest
To see the funny side, I tried my best

Gang laughed, until throats were sore
Me pride was wounded, to its very core
In sodden clothes, I squelched my way
Home to me Ma, for a hot cup o'tay

Finglas Shamrock

The Shamrock, was a well liked pub
Next to Casino, foundations did rub
No women in bar, back in the day
Somewhat outdated, women would say

Pipes and fags, hung from men's mouths
In deep conversation, drinking stouts
Talking football, or about the horse races
Knowing looks, upon the drinkers faces

A male sanctuary, with distractions none
Where men bonded, while having fun
Me cousin Tony, worked behind the bar
A lovely fella, and he pulled a mean jar

Case was taken, to end men only rules
So ladies might sit, on sacred bar stools
Times were changing, court case was won
Now lads remember, bad language none

The Drake Inn

Originally Floods, renamed the Drake Inn
Spit on me Dickie, always gave me a grin
Ireland's first, purpose-built cabaret venue
Had great performers, but a limited menu

Paddy McKiernan, was a man of vision
Made Drake his flagship, good decision
Buying the Village Inn, and Duck Inn too
With these three pubs, his empire grew

Cabaret nights, were happy nights spent
Of fun times there, I could talk at length
Frankie Vaughan and Matt Munro came
And many other stars, with similar fame

Brendan Grace, and Sonny Knowles too
Red Hurley, Tony Christy, to name a few
Dickie Rock, ladies' hearts did he steal
While enjoying, a chicken in basket meal

The Drake Inn, holds a place in our hearts
Memories of first dates, and romantic starts
A part of Finglas history, we couldn't save
Appreciate all the memories, that you gave

Cream on Top

Wake from slumber, to a familiar sound
Milkman outside, is doing his round
Clip clop, clip clop, horseshoes clang
Bringing milk, to the Plunkett Road gang

Crates rattle noisily, over every bump
It's time to get up, you lazy lump
Squeaky gate announces, milk is here
The cream on top, will be mine no fear

Bottles clang, as he delivers by hand
On the porch, like soldiers they stand
Front door opens, to a fresh new morn
To silver top bottles, cream does adorn

Remember the cream, atop of the milk
Taking that sip, it going down like silk
Who drank the cream? comes the shout
Wasn't me I answer, wiping me mouth

Did milk taste better, I remember it so
Cream on top, is what did it you know
Bring back the bottle, with silky cream
Treasure within, the small birds dream

Finglas Way Back When

Tin Church at Cappagh

My Holy Communion, I remember it still
Made in tin chapel, top of Cappagh hill
Me and me twin Brian, in that area grew
Confirmation also, we made there too

New caps, new shirts, and black shoes
Overcoats, suits, our mam did choose
Two sets of each, she bought you see
Spent a fortune, suiting up him and me

Thanks Ma and Da, for sacrifices made
Memories of both days, will never fade
Who got most money, both got the same
Twin still has his, not me, what a shame

The Christmas Feast

Christmas time, for me as a child
Was a happy place, if a little wild
Money was scarce, but fun was not
Contented, with what little we got

Turkey prepared, Xmas bells rang
Ma in the kitchen, carolers sang
Prep fresh turkey, pull out its gut
Baste it all over, and into oven put

Stuffing made, of parsley and sage
Or a recipe, from a magazine page
Crackers placed, beside each plate
Contents within, you'd love or hate

Juice from boiled ham, it was used
To boil veggies, were both infused
Juice also got used, to seal the deal
Making gravy, to smoother our meal

Prawn cocktail, added a bit of posh
Christmas table, had the finest nosh
Jelly trifle, was served at feasts end
Excited anticipation, to kids did lend

A family scramble, for comfiest seats
Plonk by telly, watch movie repeats
Belts loosened, as we all flop down
In tummy contentment, we all drown

Finglas Way Back When

Frozen Milk Bottles

Winters remembered, as a young lad
Were bitter cold, they were pretty bad
As a milk boy, I was out in all sorts
Delivering milk, to the city and ports

Milk back then, was in bottles of glass
It's how it reached, the people on mass
To frozen bottles, my fingers did stick
No gloves to protect, from winters kick

Once I slipped, glass cutting me deep
In lots of pain, I watched blood seep
At works end, I was dropped for me bus
Ladies bus waiting, over me made a fuss

I was only thirteen, just a slip of a lad
Women agreed, cart driver was a cad
Ma got angry, when she saw me hand
If I see that fecker, a punch I will land

Cut needed stitches, the hand did heal
One more tale, from my memory reel
Left Merville, for work with better pay
Another story, I shall relate another day

Tree Climbing

Homework done, boredom to heal
Meet up with pals, after your meal
Climbing trees, nobody made a fuss
Health & Safety, meant nothing to us

Freedom, games of hide and seek
Count to fifty, don't you dare peek
Bush berries, field mushrooms too
Collected and eaten, guess by who

A Silverspoon swim, and a bank dive
On summer days, 'twas great to be alive
Catching pinkeens, jam jars in hand
Show off to the girls, do a handstand

Nature provided, our fun as a child
Fresh open air, us kids running wild
Gaming for hours, until it got dark
Finglas fields, were our Jurassic Park

Swings on Lampposts

Ring A Ring A Rosie, all fall down
At blind man's Bluff, act the clown
Nick-Knack, on a neighbours door
Games of hopscotch and plenty more

On Lampposts, we'd put up a swing
Race bike wheels, we would bring
Hide and Seek, find the girl or boy
Kick the Can, empty tin was our toy

Games a plenty, which one to choose
At some you win, at others you loose
A game of soccer, what team to pick
Out on the street, we'd tackle and kick

To win at marbles, line them in a row
Swing a Conker, hit with a mighty blow
We had no mobiles, play was by touch
Tag you are it, no computers and such

Animal Mad

Pets were a plenty, in our house
Cages held, many a white mouse
Brian me Da, and Brian me brother
Were animal hoarders, like no other

Tortoise, goldfish, budgies did nest
Me brother loved animals, with a zest
He defo inherited it, from me Da
No way in heaven, was it from me Ma

She shouted at him, nearly every week
Bringing home animals, sick and meek
A myxomatosis rabbit, even one day
Ma she went crazy, no way could it stay

He had hamsters, gerbils, rabbits too
Some dogs also, he brought home a few
He kept pigeons, in a back garden loft
Ma let him, she must have gone soft

Me Da bred greyhounds, out the back
Compound he built, with a small shack
He also kept ferrets, he enjoyed a hunt
Rabbits from holes, his ferrets did shunt

Fair to say, they were both animal mad
When I think about it, in a way I'm glad
It is said a bit of madness, keeps you sane
I believe that to be true, well in the main

Cabra Baths

Finglas and Cabra, shared an open-air pool
We all went there, on holliers from school
It was on the border, the Silverspoon beside
Imaginary peace line, where gangs did reside

Great was the play, on hot summer days
Around the pool, us kids would laze
A dive bomb a belly flop, wasn't a crime
Towel whips common, a dozen a dime

The Cabra Baths, was well used by many
Plenty a young kid, in pool spent a penny
Gang consisted, of both girls and boys
Some were going out, some otherwise

Down back road, over Silverspoon bridge
Up by the Quarry, to top of the ridge
Me nicks and a sambo, wrapped in a towel
Chlorine in the water, on the eyes was foul

Suntan lotion, we never used it you see
Sunburned and blistered, that was me
Great memories, of innocence in the sun
Plenty of fun and craic, negatives none

Caps for me Gun

Knock knock, you coming out to play
I'll ask me ma, see what she'll say
She said it's ok, I'll go get me gun
Disappointment, as caps I had none

Ma I need money, for caps from shop
Here's tuppence son, don't let it drop
Gun now loaded, we start our game
Onwards to victory, to glory and fame

Bang bang you're dead, more to follow
In their blood, the baddies did wallow
Stench of cap Sulphur, filled the air
The smell of battle, you had to be there

Caps run out, a quick change of barrel
Behind me crept, a sneaky Ger Farrell
Turning quickly, I go down on one knee
Bang bang I got you, you can't kill me

He moans in pain, falls to the ground
Plugging him again, till death he found
Still got caps left, more baddies to kill
I jump to me feet, heart pumping still

Pals are in trouble, I race to their aid
Barrel a blazing, those baddies paid
Game over, we head home for our tea
Enemies no longer, all friends now we

Escaping Reality

Come weekend, to the pictures we'd go
Before Superquinn, it was the Cas you know
A few coppers to enter, more for sweets
Two flicks to watch, were our weekly treats

We watched our heroes, on the big screen
Escaping reality, engrossed in a scene
Batman the series, was in black and white
All wanted to be, Bruce the Dark Knight

Cowboy flicks, our hero was John Wayne
We lost count, of the Indians he'd slain
Science Fiction, with monsters from space
Cowering in our seats, horror on our face

Count Dracula, he filled hearts with fear
Peeking through fingers, till coast was clear
Heading home, reenacting what we'd seen
Think about next weeks, pics on the screen

Going on the Mitch

Ever skip school, as a child
Go on the mitch, go a little wild
Hide schoolbags, in a safe place
Head up the fields, at a fast pace

A secret hideaway, we had built
We kept it tidy, free from filth
In the bushes, it was well hidden
To reveal it, that was forbidden

A Huck Finn tale, for kids our age
New adventures, on every page
One day's escape, from our school
Where teachers, with canes did rule

An imaginary world, all our own
Strong memories, there were sown
The things we saw, the stuff we did
Mischief we got up to, when a kid

Let's Play Pretend

Mammies and Daddies we used to play
When stuck indoors, on a rainy day
Lay the table, with imaginary food
Do as you are told and don't be rude

It's time for bed, do as you are told
I'll give you a smack, if you are bold
Go to sleep, and turn off the light
No messing in bed, and don't you fight

It's gas the things, that gave us fun
There were no limits, absolutely none
At doctors and nurses, caring for the sick
Imaginary needles, in arms we did stick

Take your temperature, wipe your head
Check pulse, make sure you are not dead
Always playing, boredom what was that
To our energy and vigour, I raise me hat

Me Bedroom Fortress

Under the blankets, in my domain
In this hidden world, I did reign
A fortress built, for a brave King
Of his exploits, people will sing

Those hideaways built, in our bed
Imaging scenarios, inside our head
Under the blankets, safe from harm
Many the idea, our minds did farm

A bedroom fortress, just for you
Where it would lead, you never knew
The battery torch, that gave you light
That scared away, the dark of night

You a warrior, in your castle keep
While in other beds, siblings sleep
For adventures, we opened our mind
To take us places, of differing kind

A child's mind, is a wonderous thing
You could be anything, even a King
O to travel back, just once more
To my fortress, behind bedroom door

A Scout Never to Be

Joined Finglas scouts, with a grin
For merit badges, I hoped I'd win
Learn new knots, the don'ts and do's
To earn a badge, was no easy cruise

Weekend away, learn to make a fire
Try as I might, flames did expire
No fire produced, to cook the spuds
In a big field, surrounded by woods

Pitching a tent, for shelter at night
Total disaster, tent looked a fright
I wasn't cut out, for a scouting life
Didn't even own, a Swiss army knife

Use a compass, find east and west
Failed at that, is there an easier test
Folding a flag, first lay it out flat
Didn't quite master it, that was that

Attempted more, failed at them all
Time was up, I had hit a brick wall
Que Serra Serra, a scout never to be
The scouting life, just didn't suit me

Summer Holliers

A hollier destination, wasn't by plane
Cost of a flight, was totally insane
Nearer to home, hollier's we'd book
Here are some places, we were took

Picnics, were a great family day out
By the sea or a river, out and about
Head to Phoenix Park, watch the deer
Or to Dublin Zoo, that was also near

Caravan holidays, were also a treat
In Costa Del Rush, family we'd meet
Loughshinny, Skerries, add to the list
Holliers were blessed, and Sun kissed

Now it's abroad, several times a year
Flights now inexpensive, not very dear
I loved them holliers, closer to home
But I also like Malaga, Paris and Rome

Me Favorite Toy

Growing up in Finglas, as a young boy
Gun and holster, were my favorite toy
Did you have a favorite, as a child
And did your imagination, also run wild

Bang bang I shouted, bang bang again
On an invisible horse, ridden by Ken
Indians try to scalp me, on the street
Me and me posse, Indians did defeat

Kids imaginations, totally ran wild
Fondly remembered, by my inner child
Our imaginations, took us to any place
Boy the adventures, daily we did face

My imaginary horse, I rode with pride
Hi Ho Silver, in many battles I cried
We'd trot on home, at the end of play
For the supper, and chat about me day

A Bad Education

Education began, at St Bridget's school
Nuns in black habits, in class did rule
Like giant Penguins, in black and white
Scared me so much, in pants I did shite

Moved next, to the school next door
St Fergals, it even scared me more
School taught, with canes and straps
No not classrooms, just misery traps

Queuing in line, for a punishment due
Sticks in me head, six whacks for you
Pain inflictors, sure that's all they were
Some teachers good, most didn't care

Colaiste Eoin, ended me education path
The teachers there, made sure of that
Smacking heads, and other such stuff
I left, as this student had had enough

Apprenticeship, me Ma got me you see
So I left the system, that had tortured me
Methods have changed, since my day
Pain inflictors gone, I'm happy to say

Finglas Olympians

Remember our games, that energy took
We had so many, I could write a book
Those I remember, I now mention here
Are they still played, I think not I fear

Playing Hola Hoop, your hips gyrate
I tried it myself, boy did it frustrate
Handgrips, joined by a length of rope
Used for skipping, if you could cope

Game of Chase, catch me if you can
In every direction, the gang it ran
A game of football, out on the street
After school, when friends did meet

For a Tug of War, use a clothesline
Got some rope burn, sure we were fine
Around the block, the gang would race
Boy us kids, sure could move at pace

Us Finglas Olympians, I kid you not
At every game, we gave our best shot
I look back fondly, with joints that ache
If I could travel back, 40 bus I'd take

Bareback Twins

We had a riding school, near our home
In a field close by, they let horses roam
Me and me twin, would head to the field
For the riding adventures, it would yield

With sugar in pockets, and rope in hand
Up in horse field, we both would land
Horses were friendly, very easy to catch
Sugar from hands, they'd eagerly snatch

Bridles we made, from rope we brought
Placed on each horse, nice and taut
Galloping bareback, we raced each other
Who was the fastest, me or me brother

Riding bareback, it needed some skill
Wind in me face, I remember the thrill
I raise me glass, for a nostalgic toast
To the bareback twins, a memory ghost

At the Cappagh Crossing

Annunciation church, once it did tower
No longer reflecting, its once held power
Confirmation, Communion, I made there
In the tin church, before big one was there

Brides and Grooms, have walked her aisle
Her spire could be seen, for many a mile
Soon to be demolished, that is a shame
Purpose served, low attendance the blame

It was too big, and a little worse for wear
Her flock had dwindled, not many there
Remember Sundays, when church was full
Church today, doesn't have the same pull

Fond memories in church, I have a few
Times are changing, catholic church knew
In her day, she was some sight to behold
Now she awaits, a new story to unfold

Sweets I Loved to Eat

I loved me sweets, I tell you it's true
They fed me sweet tooth, as I grew
I'd spend every penny, buying treats
As young kids, we loved our sweets

Bounty, Kit Kat, side order of Twix
Rolo a Twirl, add them to the mix
A Wispa a Lion Bar, boy could it roar
Curly Whirly, and much much more

Topic, Crunchie, a tasty Milky Way
Bullseyes, Caramel, I could eat all day
Alpine Toblerone, it was out on its own
Toffee Crisp, Aero, in a different zone

Have a Time Out, on a Double Decker
Or have a Picnic, there's a head wrecker
Chocolate Orange, a Star Bar for a break
Snickers, Mars bar, or a Cadbury's Flake

The mouth is watering, here as I write
Shall I give myself a treat, I think I might
I remember as kids, us stuffing our gob
As into our mouths, our sweets we'd lob

Ma's Sisters and Brothers

Me Ma had six sisters, three brothers too
Two sisters upped sticks, to England flew
One sister Ma's twin, Lillie was her name
Not identical, they didn't look the same

May and Eileen, in England got ahead
Met Ian and Tony, who later they wed
Patty met Paddy, later taking his name
Ena met Brian, and also done the same

Sheila wed John, what a singing voice
They fell in love, had no other choice
Larry met Ana, a sister of me Da
Who introduced them, think it was Ma

Tommy met Frances, a perfect match
In Chapelizod, they bought their patch
Paddy met Maureen, had a wedding fine
Phyllis me Ma, wed me Da who is Brian

Enniskerry Weekends

To Enniskerry, with gang I'd head
For restless nights, and a lumpy bed
Pitch a tent, near woods where we slept
To chill in the river, our cider was kept

Up to all sorts, a good time our aim
Our favourite, was the drinking game
Campfire songs, cool cider to drink
Rebel songs sung, the Dubliners I think

We howled more like, none could sing
An alcohol illusion, the cider did bring
As night grew older, drink made us hazy
We got boisterous, maybe a little crazy

Cider in control, strip nearly to our nip
Swim in river, for a sobering skinny dip
Head a little clearer, not quite sober yet
Stumble to our tents, bodies a little wet

Getting up late, heads worse for wear
From the previous night, out on the tear
Do the same again, sure why the hell not
Returning the next time, to the same spot

Slave to 70's Fashion

Boyfriend was your fella, girlfriend your mot
To keep up with fashion, boy we spend a lot
Under Clerys clock, is where you met to shop
Rush in and out of stores, shop until you drop

Take a little break, go to Wimpy's for a snack
Chat about your purchase, then hurry on back
Platform shoes for him, for her platform boots
She in a mini skirt, getting whistles and hoots

A maxi a midi, or maybe a crop top vest
Hot pants, bell bottoms, which of them is best
Safari jacket, sheepskin, flared covered legs
Cardigans and sweaters, hung on clothing pegs

Drainpipe trousers, with a medallion to match
Oxford shoes, for some girls eye to catch
Winklepickers, cube heel, double breasted suit
In crushed velvet, to make you look cute

Floppy hats, kimono's, they called it casual chic
Tube tops, palazzo pants, styles girls did seek
Chokers, dog collars, were an accessory must
Hip huggers, pencil skirts, bra to boost the bust

Long hair short hair, the mullet or the shag
Mixed with good fashion, a man became a stag
Saturday Night Fever, Travolta he was to blame
At Disco nights, men dressed to ignite a flame

Snow Games

Winter months, from my distant past
Seemed for ages, that they would last
Kids were hardy, in so many ways
Or do I remember, in a nostalgic haze

Open bedroom curtains, take a peep
Snow on ground, out of bed you leap
Rush out the door, the snow to greet
Nice and crunchy, and soft under feet

Lay on your back, in the crisp snow
Making angel figures, don't you know
Build a snowman, as best you could
Add a carrot, coal, some bits of wood

Snowball fights, the battles were mad
No prisoners taken, a great time had
Make a slippery slide, out on the road
Bums getting bruised, by the cart load

Set an ambush, for unsuspecting prey
Toss your snowballs, then run away
Winter snow games, gave us such joy
Is how I remember it, when I was a boy

The Finglas Mammy

As a lad in Finglas, I bore witness to it all
The Finglas mammy, at our beck and call
From dawn to dusk, boy how they toiled
Cleaning house and clothes we had soiled

Disposable nappies, hell what were they
Nappies were cotton, back in their day
Ma's cleaned, by scraping out the shit
Placed in a basin, and let soak for a bit

Homes were heated, not by a switch
To start a home fire, it could be a bitch
Scrounge up paper, add kindling too
Turf or coal, some blowing from you

The Ma cooked meals, washed our dishes
Their home cooking, always delicious
Everything cleaned, was done by hand
Hours on their feet, our Ma's would stand

At the end of their day, they were depleted
Up early next day, same jobs got repeated
I miss her wise council, her knowing smile
The home she created, her parenting style

Mad About the Flicks

Mad about the flicks, I was in me day
We had lots of choice, I have to say
Cinemas were a plenty, in Dublin city
Most of them gone, and mores the pity

Die Hard, Bruce Willis in your face
Star Wars, took us into outer space
Exorcist, turned the head of Linda Blair
De Niro in Taxi, your worst nightmare

Brando made an offer, you couldn't refuse
In The Godfather, horse his head did lose
Saturday Night Fever, Travolta's disco feet
Danny in Grease, moved to a different beat

Blazing Saddles, Young Frankenstein too
Jaws scared the shit, out of quite a few
A Nightmare on Elm Street, blew me mind
In Apocalypse Now, Martin Sheen we find

Stepford Wife's, played the perfect role
Blood soaked Carrie, she lost control
In Close Encounters, of the Third Kind
Music communication, scientists did find

Krammer vs Krammer, a family torn apart
Jack in the Shinning, gave me such a start
Good the Bad the Ugly, that movie was wild
Damien in the Omen, was a demonic child

In Basic Instinct, and that Fatal Attraction
Michael Douglas, was in emotional traction
Alien that creature, inside John Hurts chest
Was a terrestrial intruder, an unwanted guest

Back to The Future, with Marty McFly
Terminator, I'll be back, he was a scary guy
Some great movies, impossible to mention all
Need a Ghostbuster, who you gonna call?

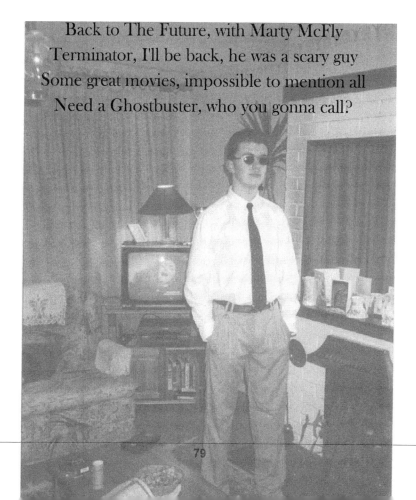

Music Growing Up

In the 60's and 70's, rock came of age
Hendricks guitar, blared out on stage
Elvis the Pelvis, with gyrating hips
The Beatles, Eagles, Mick Jagger's lips

Blondie, Kate Bush, Freddie of Queen
Springsteen, Marley, on all I was keen
Pink Floyd, The Doors, had great hits
Bowie and Elton, wore colourful kits

Sabbath, Motorhead, had heavy vibes
Halen, Zeppelin, were different tribes
Iron Maiden, Aerosmith, they had heat
Heavy rock, air guitar, experience sweet

Boomtown Rats, Van Morrison and U2
Clannad, Gallagher, were familiar too
Undertones, Thin Lizzy, Phil had style
Each one hailing, from the Emerald Isle

Sexual Healing, from Marvin Gaye
Rod the Bod, audiences did slay
Simon, Garfunkel, homeward bound
Clapton, Dylan, had a unique sound

Roxy Music, Hollies, just one look
Clash, Sex Pistols, world they shook
Jam, T. Rex, who rode the white swan
Even to this day, their music lives on

Brendan Grace had a phenomenal impact on Irish comedy and the Irish people. He was known and loved the length and breadth of Ireland. This poem is my effort at a small homage to him.

Bottler is Gone

Bottler is gone, he is on the other side
Them folks up there, are in for a ride
From naughty comic, inuendo's will fly
They'll be in stitches, on a laughter high

Grace by name, his performances too
Personas Brendan, he had quite a few
Bottler, was the best known by far
The bride's drunken dad, was also a star

Working the pubs, working the boards
His TV show, was watched by hoards
A crazed rapper priest, in Father Ted
From ghetto blaster, load music was fed

Sinatra, he was a big fan of the Grace
Invited him over, to that American place
Combine Harvester, was a Gingermen hit
This Liberties lad, he got by on his wit

Eileen his wife, was always his rock
Lifting his spirits, when he got a knock
That bright light that shone, is no more
Bottler enters, through another stage door

Ode to Phil Lynott

Phil, the boys are no longer in town
Nor your fuzzy hair, or skin of brown
It's not the same, since you're not around
Lyrics live on, in your songs and sound

Playing the Lizzy, we remember a time
Your music was poetry, in perfect rhyme
Words you wrote, revealed that raw you
A true Dub rebel, through and through

Them boys have gone, yes there gone
You left us a legacy, of wonderful song
Intolerance and passion, were your muse
Helping to ignite, the Phil Lynott fuse

With the Lizzy, you did conquer all
Climbing your Everest, only to fall
On Harry Street, stands a bronze of you
An accolade achieved, by so very few

We miss your voice, and your smile
Your boyish good looks and fashion style
An Irish rock legend, a true Dublin lad
Our rock style icon, in black leather clad

As a teenager Phil was my hero and through the years he has remained so. He and his mam Philomena, whom I had the pleasure to meet at her home in Howth, were very close. Phil was truly a proud Dubliner, from his fuzzy hair down to his winkle picker toes and Irelands greatest Rock talent.

Finglas Way Back When

Help the Halloween Party

Growing up in Finglas, I loved Halloween
In homemade costumes, we could be seen
Treats today, were only dreamt of then
If I got chocolate, I was a very happy Ken

Halloween back then, was a poorer affair
Happy with little, what people could spare
Nuts and fruit mostly, filled our bag
Give kids it today, what's that hash tag

A few loud bangers, watching the Bon fire
Throw on more pallets, maybe a car tyre
Pop in your potato, leave at edge to roast
A Halloween tradition, followed by most

Help the Halloween party, mantra at the door
Fingers crossed, hope you made a big score
Trick or Treat, just sounds all wrong today
An American infiltration, a conspiracy I say

'Twas Christmas

Christmas in Finglas, wasn't half bad
It was full of magic, I'm happy to add
Waiting for Santa, from chimney to pop
With me presents, he promised to drop

Dolls for the girls, guns for the boys
That's how it was, those were our toys
Mammies and daddies, girls would play
Us boys as cowboys, on Indians did prey

The Plunkett gang, had guns out in force
Did we play cowboys, we did of course
Chasing each other, but avoid being shot
Happy back then, with what little we got

Ham and Turkey, was our traditional fare
A mixture of veg, yes stuffing was there
Soup to begin, a tasty starter to our meal
Trifle with Cream, always sealed the deal

During dinner, came the big bang pull
With bits and bobs, crackers were full
Watch a Christmas movie, on the telly
Family content, relaxed with full belly

Thanks

I would like to take the opportunity to thank the people on the Facebook page Finglas Memories. It was them who encouraged me put these poems into this collection.

Also, I would like to thank my uncle Thomas Duffy for giving his permission for the use of the old family photographs featured throughout this book.

Finally, I wish to extend a special thank you to my wonderful daughter in law Vivian, who is married to my son Alan, for her incredible energetic input into producing this book. Without her enthusiasm, organisational skills and choreography of the graphics m book would still be just an aspirational idea.

Printed in Great Britain
by Amazon